THE WIT AND WISDOM OF VLADIMIR PUTIN

Edited and translated in part by
Daniel Sochor, BA (Russian Studies), JD

CONTENTS

There is always hope when people are forced to listen to both sides.

John Stuart Mill, *On Liberty*

I

In your family, your father fought in the war and your mother survived the blockade. Did your parents talk to you about the war when you were a child?

Vladimir Putin: Of course they did, but not very often. In general, it was not a subject we often discussed. I have a feeling that my parents did not like talking about it very much. Nevertheless, it was something we talked about, especially when marking particularly memorable events.

Do you think they were trying to protect you, or was it a painful subject for them?

Vladimir Putin: I think it was painful for them. They avoided the topic. Not least because they lost a child during the war: my brother, whom I never met. It was a tragedy, they were clearly very difficult times. That's why they did not like talking about it.

What about your personal perception of it... Naturally, this is something that changes with age... While in childhood, it is mainly shaped by war movies, etc., with age you come to understand the tragedy of it. How did your understanding of what the war and blockade really were change as you grew up?

Vladimir Putin: You know, with age I came to see those stories they told me as a child in a different light. For example, I knew that my mum visited my father in hospital after he had been wounded. My father had told me that he was with a partisan unit in the beginning of the war, but I later found out that in reality he was with a sabotage group. When I was President, I requested documents from the archives. My father was no longer alive then, he had already passed away. Amazingly, the documents tallied with everything he had told me, right down to the tiniest detail. I did learn that there were 28 of them who were sent across enemy lines to gather intelligence and carry out sabotage operations. Only four of those 28 survived. One thing that my father had never told me, something I learnt from the archives, was that the group was led by a Russian citizen of German descent.

He wasn't interned at the beginning of the war?

Vladimir Putin: I don't know. I don't know anything about that. They only gave me the archival documents, record cards, personal records, and I was surprised to learn that the group was led by an ethnic German. It was probably because he knew German. I do not know why those in charge back then made that decision. But it was new to me, it was something I knew nothing about. After that my father was sent to the front and fought at the Neva Bridgehead. He was wounded there, and my mother told me how she would visit him in hospital. My father shared his hospital food ration with her and would give her provisions. And then he started having fainting fits from starvation, as he was probably giving all his food to my mother. The hospital staff noticed this, and as sad as it may sound now, but this was the thinking back then, they banned her from visiting. They had banned her from visiting him, and this was truly tragic, when he had recovered, he went to visit her at home. He arrived as they were carrying corpses out of the building, and there among those corpses, he saw my mum. It turned out she was still alive. I will not go into all the details here, but they carried her back in and she lived. It was one thing when they told this story when I was very young. Of course I did not really understand the scale of the tragedy the city, its residents, and my relatives experienced during the war. Later, I started to see everything differently and came to understand the true meaning of the blockade, the enormous suffering and the great tragedy it was for millions of people. My understanding has certainly changed with age.

Mr Putin, what are your primary associations with the word blockade?

Vladimir Putin: The first thought that comes to mind is the tragedy of it, that it was a tragedy for a large number of ordinary citizens. The soldiers were at least fed a little better, but there was a period when civilians were on their own. They died from cold and starvation. Therefore, the blockade is above all an enormous tragedy for millions of people. On the other hand, it is also an unprecedented feat of heroism, and endurance. It was a quite remarkable feat: the amazing endurance of such a large number of people, their collective heroism.

Mr President, your brother died during the siege of Leningrad. Did you hate the Germans for this?

Vladimir Putin: I know that this caused my parents much suffering and they never forgot it, but there was never hatred towards the Germans in my family for this, strange as it may sound. My parents always said that it was not the people who were guilty, not the ordinary soldiers sent to war by the regime in power. It is not the people who carry the blame, but the ideology, in this terrible case, the ideology of national socialism.

My mother told me a story about my grandfather, who fought during the First World War. Troops on the opposing sides took up positions in trenches within sight of each other. Austrian soldiers had taken up position on the other side of the section where my grandfather was. My grandfather shot one of the

Austrians and badly wounded him. The Austrian was lying there in a pool of his own blood and no one was making any moves to come and help him. My grandfather then climbed up out of the trench, went over to him and bandaged his wound. They embraced each other before parting.

What did your parents tell you about their personal experience during World War II? How did your family greet the end of the war?

Vladimir Putin: My parents were reluctant to talk about those years. They were very difficult memories for them. They usually talked about the war only when friends and acquaintances came to our home. I was born in 1952. My parents never told me about how they greeted the end of the war, about May 8 and May 9, 1945. For them at that time it marked the end of an unimaginably difficult period in their lives. My father was wounded and was in hospital in Leningrad when the city was still besieged by the Nazi forces. At one point he came home to look for my mother and arrived right at the moment when the so-called "burial teams" were about to put her with the corpses and take her to the cemetery. But she was still alive and my father had to pull her out from under this mountain of corpses. She survived only because he gave her the rations that he was entitled to as someone who was wounded and recovering in hospital.

It is indeed here, on this patch, that my father fought... It is a small patch of land that is only 3 kilometres wide and 1.5 kilometres long. This place was the "key" to besieged Leningrad and played a very important role in the defence of the city and in breaking the blockade. Here my father really did fight, was seriously injured and then, in hospital in Leningrad, this seemingly tragic circumstance saved the life of my mother, as she was then also in the Leningrad blockade, and as they said, he fed her from his hospital rations. But they could not save their son who fell ill and died in the Leningrad blockade. This was my brother, whom I never saw. Every Leningrad family has such a loss on account of the war.

There is no disputing whatsoever that Russia is my life. That is a fact. Not for a second can I imagine myself without Russia. I've said in the past about how I looked through my family's genealogy in the archives. They all came from not far from Moscow, 120 kilometres away. There is a village where my forebears have lived since the 17th century, going all these long years to one and the same church. In this sense I feel a connection with the Russian soil and Russian people and could never live anywhere but Russia.

My father was a worker at one of Leningrad's industrial enterprises and my mother was also a worker. We lived in a communal apartment. This is an apartment shared by several families. We had one room of just over 20 square metres and with virtually no conveniences. But this was not what mattered the most. What was most important was that I always felt the love, attention and care of my parents and the people who surrounded me, and so I do not recall this time as a difficult time and do not have bad memories of it. We had the basic minimum and really, people do not need such a lot to be happy.

My mother was a believer. In the former Soviet Union it was not just unfashionable, as it is now, but it was even dangerous. And she had me baptised in church, not secretly, but without publicising the matter. I am proud to be associated with the Russian Orthodox Church. I think it is a great honour. It links me to my people, its culture, and it gives me inner calm and moral fortitude. I think it is very good.

I find it strange that you say I had a difficult childhood. It may appear so to people who lived in affluence and who enjoyed all the benefits of modern civilization. I did not have such opportunities, but I never felt disadvantaged or miserable. Basically I had the same kind of childhood as millions of Soviet – now Russian – citizens, perhaps even a better childhood in some ways. The main thing was not the material everyday conditions in which I lived, the main thing was the moral conditions. And what mattered was that everybody had affection for me. My parents were very fond of me, I have always felt that, and I am very grateful to them for that.

I first earned money when I was a member of a student construction team. We went to the Komi Republic where we cut down trees for a power transmission line to be made, and we built and repaired houses. I earned about a thousand roubles, a fantastic amount at the time. A car cost around 4000 then, I think. I must confess that I made very poor use of that money. I won't tell you how.

When I came to work in the Leningrad department of the KGB, we were planning some operation. One of our veterans said we needed to do this and this. I told him: "Listen, I think it is illegal." I was young and just out of university. They just laughed at me, thank God, it was already 1976, far from the time of repressions.

You know, my children, my daughters, despite all the rumours, live here in Russia, in Moscow. I have grandchildren and they live a normal life too. My daughters are involved in science and education and they stay out of the public eye, out of politics and live normal, everyday lives. As for my grandchildren, one of them is already in kindergarten.

The thing is, you see, I do not want them to grow up like some royal princes. I want them to live like ordinary people, and for this, they need to have a normal environment and ordinary interaction with other children. The minute I give their names and ages, they would be identified immediately and would never be left in peace, and this would be quite simply detrimental to their development. Therefore, everything is fine, and I ask you to understand me correctly and show understanding for this position of mine.

II

The strength of a leader is not measured by their handshake; it is measured by their attitude towards the work they do, towards the fate of their country and their people, and by their personal commitment and dedication.

The question is not about having a lot of power, it's about using the power that you do have in the right way.

I lived almost 30 years in a communal apartment in Leningrad, even after becoming a KGB officer. And I know very well and feel how an ordinary Russian citizen lives. It is a big advantage when making decisions, it helps. Feedback from the people is very important, you must not lose it, but it is hard to keep because technological life is such that it leads, as everyone knows, to isolation.

A decent person remains decent under the communist system and in a democratic society. And, vice versa, a dishonest person will remain dishonest in any social system.

The strength is in the truth. When a Russian feels he is right, he is invincible. I am saying this with absolute sincerity, not for the sake of just saying it. If we knew we had done something bad and were unfair, then everything would be hanging by a thread.

Every person has a talent, but not everyone gets the chance to reveal it. Self-accomplishment is what I'd like to wish for every one of us.

Freedom ends where we start transgressing on the freedom of other people.

The law has to be obeyed at all times, and not just when they've grabbed you by your private parts.

As a child, I spent most of my time playing in the street, in the courtyard in the centre of Leningrad, a large city. Boys my age spent most of their time there. This was a sort of "university" and a school of life. I will not go into details, but one such vivid memory I have is – let me put it this way – my incorrect behaviour towards a person and his abrupt response. This happened several times; but it is a thing you can learn from, and you learn not just to be polite to other people but to have respect for them.

How do you handle aggression directed towards you? Do you allow yourself to be aggressive towards other people?

Vladimir Putin: Aggression has been part of our make-up since prehistoric times, when our ancestors were in an animal or semi-animal state. However, the more intelligent and the more educated people are, the less aggressive they are. In any case, they are much better at controlling it. Of course, I constantly run into stressful situations, I do not like many things, but I learned to restrain myself. I am not sure how it looks from the outside, but I think that I am good at it. Moreover,

I believe that this is a great advantage in dealing with people, especially ones who cannot control these emotions. I may fly off the handle occasionally, which is extremely rare, and, frankly, I get very angry with myself when it happens, because I believe that the manifestation of aggression in today's world, in today's society, in relations between people is a manifestation of weakness. I do not like this. When there are no arguments left to make, a person begins to behave aggressively. Overall, I manage to cope with it, which is what I wish for you, too.

What was the happiest and the most unusual moment in your life?

Vladimir Putin: This is not an easy question. Could you answer it yourself if you were asked the same question? There are a lot of happy moments, so it is really hard to tell which one was the happiest. As a general rule, these moments are usually related to achievements, victories and life choices. These are the moments you remember, so I think that even if a victory is small, it still matters, since it helps shape a person's character and identity. For example, I remember competing one time in some tournament at a pretty basic level. It may not seem like such a remarkable event, but it was then that I first started believing in myself, and finally understood that I have the ability to overcome many challenges. There have been quite a few moments of this kind in my life. I hope that more are to come, and I would wish this to be case for all of you.

One ancient eastern sage said: "It is easy to love the whole world, just try to love your neighbour."

I think we should not slap children and justify it based on some old traditions. Neither parents, nor neighbours should do this, although this sometimes happens. There is a short distance from slaps to beating. Children fully depend on adults; they are the most dependent members of society. There are many other ways to bring children up without slapping.

I have been practising the Asian martial arts for my entire life, and I have a philosophy for relating to a partner. No matter who he is, he must be treated with respect. This philosophy is based on both general human considerations and pragmatism. If we think that we are surrounded by some small fry that are not worthy of our attention, we may take some unexpected hits, and very painful ones at that.

If you are afraid of a dog, it will bite you some day, but if you behave as its owner, it will wag its tail. This is how we should behave in dealing with [terrorist] criminals.

There is no hiding behind your teammates in martial arts. Whether in the ring, or on the mat or the tatami, there is only you and the opponent, and it means a lot to take victory in an uncompromising and honest fight.

You know what they say among the Russian people, "Those who are destined to be hanged, are not going to drown." Only God knows our destiny. The question is what we will have accomplished by then in this transient world, and whether we will have enjoyed our life.

As one famous figure said, a good politician thinks about elections, but a good statesman thinks about future generations.

The more you do, the more things you can do within a given amount of time. Especially if you organise your work schedule really well. Believe me, that is the way it is.

Mr President, I have a young daughter. When she flips through the channels in search of cartoons she looks at programmes and asks me questions. Recently she asked me: "Dad, who is Putin?" How would you explain to a little child who the President is?

Vladimir Putin: He is a person who works to make you happy. This is what he works and lives for.

In principle, I love travelling. But all my travels are now limited to driving to an airport, flying somewhere and then back to the airport, and this is it, the trip is over. I would like to travel differently, to enjoy nature or see historical monuments.

I never get personal. Never, because practice and experience show that personal contacts can always come in handy when settling relations between states or in resolving issues that affect millions of people. Therefore, one should leave any personal ambitions to oneself, for safekeeping.

Those who regularly go to the gym understand all the advantages of keeping fit. Movement is life.

I recently had a conversation with a friend of mine from Europe, who is a big boss there. After all that happened last year, he asked: "Listen, is there love in your life?" And I said: "What do you mean?" He said, "Is there anyone you love?" I said, "Well, sure." "And does someone love you?" I replied "Yes." He must have thought I was neglected. So he said "Thank God," and drank a shot of vodka. So everything is fine, don't worry.

We have this very old joke about a pessimist and an optimist: a pessimist drinks his cognac and says, "It smells of bedbugs," while an optimist catches a bedbug, crushes it, then sniffs it and says, "A slight whiff of cognac." I would rather be the pessimist who drinks cognac than the optimist who sniffs bedbugs.

The most important thing in any sphere of activity is to feel that you are a professional and to constantly increase your level of expertise and the quality of your work.

I am a pragmatist with a conservative perspective.

When I, as someone who grew up on the streets of Leningrad, hear about something elitist, I always find myself immediately feeling suspicious towards it, because I get the feeling that is something beyond the reach of ordinary citizens, something cut off from citizens and from the people.

Decisions must be made soberly and coolly, but making them is impossible without any emotion. I think about how they will affect the average citizen. I remember how my father walked out onto the landing and carefully read the electric meter. You know, our older generation is precise, meticulous. They may have been pennies, but he wrote down every penny, every kilowatt, and always made these payments on time. And it was important for the family. And I remember all of this – how he went up the ladder and read the meter. This is life – the real lives of ordinary families. We must never forget that.

Trust is the most important component of power and it is something I value immensely. I am very grateful to people for feeling that I really have spent these last eight years working honestly, toiling like a galley slave every day. And I see that there are also people who do not see things in this way, who do not perceive it as I do, but I do not blame them for this, I blame myself for not having managed to reach out properly to these people. This means I did not work hard enough and could have done more. But overall, what I am most grateful for is people's trust.

A foreign language is not just a gateway to communication, it is a gateway to the culture of another people. It is very interesting, it opens up a whole world. In fact, having a second language is like living another life.

I think one should most be guided in one's activities, not by the opinion of other people, but rather by one's own conscience.

I would recall Roosevelt who led the country in a period of grave crisis. I think it was not by chance that he broadcast his 'fireside chats', talking at length to the country's people. I think his genius, like that of de Gaulle and Erhard, was that they felt what needed to be done, they felt the mood of their people and tried to be on the same wavelength as the people, and they did it very well.

The person at the top of the power pyramid should never forget that he should act in such a way as to be able tomorrow to live in this country, look people honestly in the eye and recall fondly the times when he was taking decisions on which the fates of millions of people depended.

I never take arbitrary decisions, decisions that may entail consequences I can't foresee. And if I can't foresee the consequences, I prefer to take some time. It's like overtaking another car on the road: never try unless you are certain.

In order to work with people effectively you have to be able to establish a dialogue and bring out the best in your partner. If you want to achieve results you have to respect your partner. And to respect means to recognise that he is in some way better than you are. You should make that person an ally, make him feel that there is something that unites you, that you have some common goals.

I know that some leaders in other countries, even US presidents, once worked in intelligence. I served my country and I did it honestly and I have nothing to repent about. And I must say that, strange though it may sound, I have never broken the laws of other countries.

I enjoy reading Russian classics, especially Dostoevsky and Tolstoy. I am fond of Hemingway. I used to really love Saint-Exupery. I memorised "The Little Prince" by heart.

I am absolutely certain that for someone involved in politics willpower is the most important quality. People who have no willpower are just experts. They may be good experts or bad experts, but they are specialists who can only give advice. Without willpower you cannot make decisions.

If you behave in a disorganised and lax fashion, this spreads down the chain of command. It sends the wrong signal to the whole government. So you have to be tough and demanding.

If a person in power feels that they have lost the bond connecting them to the country and to the rank and file citizens of the country, then it's time for them to go.

There are opponents in the ring, on the mat and on the tatami. But there are no enemies. Wouldn't it be wonderful if it was always like that, in life as well?

Am I a 'pure democrat'? Of course I am, absolutely. The problem is that I'm all alone, the only one of my kind in the whole wide world. There has been no one to talk to since Mahatma Gandhi died.

It is not a question of a strong figure, although a strong figure is needed in power, it is a question of what is implied by this term.

Of course the Government should always be criticized. Criticism helps to look at things from a different perspective, which is always good.

You can't make everyone your ally and you shouldn't even strive to do it. On the contrary, it's good to have around some people who have doubts.

The point of conservatism is not that it obstructs movement forward and upward, but that it prevents movement backward and downward.

It is easy to promise everyone housing, happiness, health and wealth tomorrow but this is idle talk and it is unfair.

Long discussions and deliberations about how things could be done better, and failure to act at a time when fast decision-making is needed, are more dangerous than taking action, even if it is imperfect.

The President cannot go beyond the Constitution of the Russian Federation. But sometimes the temptation to do so is great.

When a person stays in power too long, even if he is a very good person, his incentives are blunted, he doesn't have "fire in his belly", like at the start of the journey. Secondly, he comes to be surrounded by all sorts of groups, which are known as the camarilla.

Responsibility must always be personal.

Nobody, no government, can dictate to an artist, a writer, a film director, or actually to any person what kind of creative work gifted people should do and in what way. Often, they see something that was once considered unacceptable and today is a standard in their own new way.

There is elite wine, there are elite resorts. There are no elite people.

It is not only fear that drives people, sometimes it is conscience.

Breakdancing truly promotes a healthy lifestyle, because it is difficult to imagine how it could be related to drug use. It would be impossible to perform especially when you see the acrobatics some of these guys do. This really does command respect.

If we have made a promise to the people, then we must deliver on that promise. Otherwise it is better not to make such promises in the first place.

You shouldn't wait for some good guys to do something for you. You have to fight for your rights.

I think every person must have a moral and spiritual core. It does not matter what denomination he belongs to.

All of us – young people and older people – must be efficient. The state as a whole must be more efficient. It depends on how well we adapt to the new living conditions. We should remember what happened to the dinosaurs.

When life sets us certain challenges, we are forced to tackle them one way or another and we do.

Everything will probably never be all right. But we will aspire to it.

III

We have a famous poem, which goes: "You will not grasp her with your mind or cover with a common label, for Russia is one of a kind – believe in her, if you are able."

What in your opinion impedes Russia's development most of all?

Vladimir Putin: One can philosophise on that score endlessly. In the sphere of mentality, of course, it is the socialised consciousness, the expectation that the state should solve all the problems. That of course restricts individual initiative.

An ordinary Russian person had nothing of his own and permanently worked for his master. So, what was left over for him was a blessing, and he knew that they could snatch away everything. It all stems from the times of serfdom. There could have been no proper attitude to current affairs, business and property. It had not been formed like it had in the countries with a developed market system, where a person is aware that he must struggle for his own wealth and for his family's.

The simpler the person is, the closer he is to his roots, the more responsible he feels for his Motherland. He is not going to either board a plane, train or mount a horse to leave or buzz off from here. Yes, those who have billions feel like global citizens. They feel more free, particularly if their money is in offshore banking accounts. They have gone abroad and stay there, feeling good.

Gorbachev took the first step and Yeltsin completed what I think was a historic and very important transition for Russia and its people. Both of them, Yeltsin above all, of course, gave Russia freedom, and this is indisputably the historic achievement of the Yeltsin era. The tragedy is that people's hopes were disappointed because freedom to do as one pleased was called democracy, and the theft of millions to enrich a few, the plunder of immense resources that belonged to the whole people, was called the market and market relations.

In my country if a person steals a bag of potatoes he's a thief. If a person steals hundreds of millions of dollars, he's a political figure and can't be touched.

How do you account for the brain drain from our country and what specifically is being done to slow it down or stop it?

Vladimir Putin: First of all, if brains leave the country, at least you can say that there are brains to begin with. And that already is good news. Secondly, it means that they are good quality brains because otherwise there wouldn't have been any drain. That is also good news. It shows the high standard of training. Third, if we want to see our economy integrated into the world economy we should welcome the free movement of people, capital, labour, and so on. Capital and skills will inevitably flow where they find better conditions for their application. This is the law of the market.

It used to be said that Russia had two big problems – roads and fools. I think that we have two other big problems today – incompetence and corruption.

The line that separates opposition activists from the fifth column is hard to see from the outside.

Do you remember an anecdote when one family comes to visit another family and they ask their guests: "Do you take your tea with sugar?" - "Yes, with sugar." - "Well, then, you will have to wash your hands without soap." You may laugh at it but it seems that people were thinking that things could not get any worse. We all have to understand that once revolutionary changes, not evolutionary, but revolutionary changes begin, things can become worse, much worse.

Let me remind you of something that Stolypin said: "I hope that Russia will be able to distinguish blood on the hands of a doctor from blood on the hands of an executioner." By the way, you know, there is no death penalty in Russia today.

Do you remember the old joke where one person asks, "How is your health?" and the other answers, "Don't waste your time waiting."

Only a small group of people are involved in writing laws, while millions are working on ways to evade them.

The number of persons prosecuted for corruption has been growing steadily. It is not because there are more crimes – it is because more crimes are being exposed.

Things are changing very slowly here. The presumption of guilt is still very much alive.

Do not confuse democracy with anarchy.

Total calm can be achieved only in a cemetery. And where there are living people, there are clashes of opinions and views, and there is nothing strange about it.

The Soviet Union became embroiled in a futile war, a war that lasted almost 10 years. And today we are duty-bound to analyse and draw lessons from the Afghan war and face the truth. The Afghan war proved that no one has the right to interfere in the life of another country and neither communism, nor democracy, nor a market economy can be imposed by force.

We should not follow the path of blindly copying what other countries are doing. We should understand what is going on there, analyse the situation, find the best practices and implement them in our country.

If there is no money, what can you do? You can't go to the store, you can't buy anything, neither a gun, nor a missile, nor medicine. For this reason the economy is at the basis of everything.

When the economy goes into crisis, people say that the state needs to take control of this or take that. As soon as the economy recovers from the crisis, people say that state regulation is just a set of shackles.

Russia expanded territorially the most under Catherine. In this sense she was a more efficient monarch than Peter the Great: less blood and more acquisition.

It was Stalin who once said that it is not whom people vote for that matters, but who does the counting. I hope though, that this will not be the case.

D. Grishin [CEO Mail.ru]: There is a preconception that any contact with the authorities, in general, will not lead to anything good.

Vladimir Putin: That's right. (Laughter.)

D. Grishin: In principle, if you can hide and suppose they won't notice, it's better to hide.

Vladimir Putin: That's not right. First of all, it makes no difference, there is nowhere you can hide from us. (Laughter.) Secondly, it's simply unworthy for representatives of such a promising business as yours to hide from somebody. Why do so? You have to crawl out from under a rock and associate with people. However unpleasant it is, you have to get together with society and the government and search for common solutions.

We do not have the [surveillance] capabilities the US has at its disposal. If we had, then maybe we would be just as bad.

Mr Yeltsin invited me to come and see him and said that he wanted to offer me the prime minister's job. Incidentally, he never used the word 'successor' in his conversation with me then, but spoke of becoming 'prime minister with prospects', and said that if all went well, he thought this could be possible. I thought then, if I can get through a year that will already be a good start. If I can do something to help save Russia from falling apart then this would be something to be proud of.

I didn't know what President Yeltsin's final plans were with regard to me. At any moment the President could tell me, "You're fired." And there was only one thing I was thinking about, "Where to hide my children."

The less our officials and heads of major companies go abroad and work on pressing matters instead, the better. The same is true of State Duma deputies, who need to communicate more frequently with their voters, rather than tanning somewhere at foreign resorts.

Russia is not claiming great power status. It is a great power by virtue of its huge potential, its history and culture.

He who does not regret the destruction of the Soviet Union has no heart, and he who wants to see it recreated in its former shape has no brain.

I am prepared to talk to everyone who really aims to improve people's lives, to resolve the issues facing the country, but not the ones who use existing difficulties to promote their own political agenda. Using difficulties as a tool for self-promotion and in order to cash in politically, only aggravates them. Instead, they should offer solutions. Those who offer solutions deserve our closest attention.

There is a famous Soviet-era joke, when an HR manager says: We are not going to promote this guy. Why? He had an incident with a fur coat. It turned out that five years ago his wife's fur coat was stolen in a theatre. Something had happened, so the guy will not be promoted, just in case. This should not be our attitude.

Those who oppose us try to take a bite out of those at the top because it always raises their own rating. They jump out of their pants and get into fights, but they must be careful about it because, as they say in the country, you can lose your pants if you're not careful.

For lawyers the more laws the better: you earn more fees from clients because they get completely confused by all these laws.

When he brought up cases of theft, Peter the Great suggested that people be sent to Siberia or executed for even those minor crimes. But the General Prosecutor said to him, "Who will be left, Sire? We all steal."

What is the difference which ethnic group an offender belongs to? It is pointless and even harmful to mention it.

When a spy came to the KGB to give himself up he was asked: "Do you have a weapon?" He says: "Yes". "Then go to such and such room. And do you have means of communication? Then go to room number 5. And money?" "Yes". "Then go to room 7." And when he arrives, they ask him again: "Do you have an assignment?" "Yes". "Then go and do your work, don't bother people here who are going about their business." It was the highest manifestation of bureaucracy.

We need to understand that these [law-enforcement] agencies are entrusted with a vital state function and we must not treat them like dirt; otherwise our liberal intelligentsia will have to shave off their beards, don their helmets and go out onto the streets and squares to fight the radicals.

It's our culture: when a guy gets a license or some "stick" in his hands, he immediately begins to swing it and try to make money using it. But this applies not only to the police but in every area where people have authority and the opportunity to make illegal money.

If I see that people go into the streets not just to talk or promote themselves but to say something important and relevant and draw the government's attention to some problem, there is nothing wrong with that. I will thank them.

Democracy and law and order always go hand in hand. Rule of law is impossible without democracy, but democracy is impossible without adherence to the law.

Recently there have been a lot of cases where corruption has come to light. But I consider that this is good. You know how bad it would be if people in Russia felt that they were surrounded by corruption and not by the prosecution of corruption.

Of course, a court and a prosecutor's office are not places which give awards, certificates, orders, medals and cash prizes. The prosecutor's position is that cash prizes have already been received, and it is necessary to find out whether they were received legally.

Individuals can build on their capabilities only in a free society. And if they are able to do so, they contribute to the development of the country, its science, its industry, taking it to the highest possible level. Otherwise, society stagnates.

[On Pussy Riot] Some fans of group sex say it's better than one-on-one because, like in any teamwork, you don't need to hit the ball all the time.

There is a joke, which goes like this: "Doctor, you have pulled out my healthy tooth. "Never mind, we'll get to the sick one in due course." I don't think it would be right if we proceed in this way.

The extent to which people trust the state depends directly on how well the state protects them from the arbitrary actions of racketeers, bandits and bribe takers.

The communist idea is no more than a beautiful and to some extent harmful fairy-tale.

Each of us may become something of a magician on the night of the New Year. To do this we simply need to treat our parents with love and gratitude, take care of our children and families, respect our colleagues at work, nurture our friendships, defend truth and justice, be merciful and help those who are in need of support. This is the whole secret.

I will remind you that 2017 has been declared the Year of the Environment, and environmental protection has been included in the recently approved National Science and Technology Development Strategy as a priority. It is clear that this policy is for the long term – for the next 20, 30 years or more. But, unless we start moving, we will go in circles forever complaining that we do not have enough money to address the current issues, and we will never get around to strategic issues. We cannot delay this any longer.

Everyone wants to run commercials on their channels. To be able to run the commercials you need to have an audience. The audience of the channels is counted, and a television company gets paid for running ads depending on the audience. I am giving you a general idea of how it works. Therefore, all they show are gangsters and police. That's all there is to it.

I remember well my visit to Kresty [a pre-trial detention centre in St Petersburg]. True, this was many years ago, but people were getting teeth removed there without receiving any anaesthetic. What kind of situation is this? What century are we living in? I hope that nothing of this sort is going on today.

The country is going through very hard times, what is your forecast for the future?

Vladimir Putin: Two friends meet and one asks the other: "How are you?" The other says: "My life is all stripes, black stripes followed by white ones." - "So which one is it now?" - "Now I'm in the black one." Another six months pass, they meet again: "How's life? I know it's all stripes, but which one is it now?" - "It's black now." - "But it was black last time!" - "Looks like it was white last time."

It is impossible to solve the health problems of millions of people with the help of pills. People need to put into practice and have a passion for a healthy lifestyle, fitness and sports.

Life expectancy is increasing, but for men it is 65 and a half years, and setting the retirement age for men at 65 means that, pardon me for this straightforward expression: you've done your fair share, here's your wooden overcoat, have a nice ride? That's impossible.

People should spend their money on gym memberships rather than on partying with friends.

We make families of the traditional kind our priority. But this does not mean that we are going to persecute people of non-traditional orientation.

As one close acquaintance of mine said, "The best expression of patriotism is not to steal."

We cannot make these amnesties too frequent otherwise there won't be anyone left in the prisons.

Can you tell me what the big difference is between Cromwell and Stalin? There is none. From the point of view of the liberal part of our political establishment, they are both bloody dictators. The former was actually a very cunning man who played a somewhat controversial part in the history of Britain; however, his monument is there, nobody is tearing it down.

People woke up one day, and the country [Soviet Union] was gone – and nobody asked them. They suddenly realised they were living abroad. All sorts of things started happening, including ethnic conflicts. People found themselves in a crisis, often without work, without any prospects for the future.

The fact of the matter is that we did not produce anything that people actually demanded. No one bought the galoshes we produced except in Africa, to wear them in the hot sand.

Only one thing is unacceptable: to serve the interests of a foreign state with regard to Russia.

It's not just the question of elites; in society, there are always some kinds of bacillus that destroy this social or public organism. But they become active when the immunity decreases, when problems arise, when the mass of people, millions of people, begin to suffer.

One can endlessly speculate on the tragedy of the Chechen people during their deportation from Chechnya by Stalin's regime. But were Chechens the only victims of repression? The first and the biggest victim was the Russian nation, which suffered the most as a result of repression. This is our common history.

We do have bleak chapters in our history; just look at events starting from 1937. And we should not forget these moments of our past. All states and peoples have had their ups and downs through history.

Someone is writing poetry, and someone is in Siberia. "Someone is in prison, and Vasilyeva is walking around her posh apartment" and so on. You know, just because some are in prison, especially if they were imprisoned wrongfully, does not mean that Ms Vasilyeva and others like her should be imprisoned too.

Eavesdropping is not good, I learned this during my time working for the KGB, so I don't do that.

What we are seeing is like wild capitalism letting out another belch.

When you started talking about maths, I remembered a well-known joke from back in the Soviet era: the teacher in maths class asks Givi what two plus two makes, and he replies, "Are we buying or selling?"

I believe it is my duty to protect the rights of sexual minorities, but let's face it: gay marriages do not produce children. Both Europe and Russia are facing a demographic crisis.

Often, and sometimes rightly, we criticise everything that happened in Soviet times, but I must say that quality education in the Soviet Union really did contribute to upward social mobility. I know this from my friends, my acquaintances, and my personal experience. It is well-known that I come from a working class family: my father was a blue-collar worker and my mother was simply a general labourer. Family income was extremely modest.

I was already working in the KGB, but we were still living in a shared apartment without any modern amenities. And if it were not for the opportunities the Soviet regime provided to young people like me – to get a decent education, then go abroad to work, be invited to work at a university as the rector's assistant, and then the Leningrad City Council and so on – I would have never had a chance to do all this. And perhaps today it is quite difficult to do this, and this is our common misfortune. We need to return this quality to our education – make it work as a means of social mobility.

The free circulation of firearms would cause great harm and pose a great threat for us. People have too many weapons as it is.

Do you know what the problem is with our educational system? The problem, unfortunately, is that there is a disconnect between how professionals are educated and what the labour market actually needs.

Between 1924 and 1953, when Stalin led the country, it changed dramatically: It turned from an agrarian country into an industrialized one. True, there were no peasants left and we all remember well the problems, especially in the final period, with agriculture, the food queues, etc. All that happened in the rural areas had no positive impact. But industrialisation was accomplished.

We won the Great Patriotic War. Whoever and whatever one might say, victory had been won. Even if we go back to the question of casualties, you know, nobody can today throw stones at those who organised and led us to victory because if we had lost that war, the consequences to our country would have been far more catastrophic. They are hard to imagine.

All the undeniable positive things, however, had been accomplished at an unacceptable price. Repressions did take place. It is a fact. Millions of our fellow citizens suffered from them. Such a method of running the state, of achieving results is unacceptable. It is impossible. Undoubtedly, during that period we were confronted not only with a personality cult, but with massive crimes against our own people.

In the old days we told this joke: When you ask a General: "Can a General's son become a General?" he says: "Yes, he can." "And can a General's son become a Marshal?" "No, he cannot." "Why not?" "Because Marshals have their own children."

Looking at the problems we have yet to resolve, one of the biggest is the huge income gap between the people at the top and the bottom of the scale.

And now for the most important matter. What is most important for our country? The Defence Ministry knows what is most important. Indeed, what I want to talk about is love, women, children. I want to talk about the family, about the most acute problem facing our country today – the demographic problem.

We lived for many decades in the Soviet Union under the slogan that rather than thinking about the present generation, we must think of the future one. In the end, by not thinking of the people living today, we destroyed the country.

The backwater is in many ways superior to the metropolises. There everything is more honest, more open and more transparent, and the relations among people there are often genuine and not ephemeral and prompted by concerns about career and money. If our provinces manage to preserve all that as the infrastructure and living standards improve, I think life there will change for the better.

History over the centuries, right down to modern civilisation, has proven the senselessness of the death penalty. Pickpockets in ancient Rome were sentenced to public execution, and it was precisely during these public executions that the greatest number of pockets were picked because huge crowds gathered to watch the spectacle and the pickpockets had a field day. The most effective weapon in the fight against crime is the certainty of being punished and not the severity of the punishment.

Taking wealth from the rich and giving it to the poor is the most dreadful thing that can be done. We must strengthen the institution of property.

Eighty-three percent of entrepreneurs who faced criminal charges fully or partially lost their business – they got harassed, intimidated, robbed and then released. This certainly isn't what we need in terms of a business climate.

It is not a crime to play on the currency market. Profiteers always appear when there is a chance to make some money.

We do not need to substitute all imports. Can we grow bananas? Yes. But should we? No, because they would be expensive and we can certainly buy bananas somewhere else.

There are so many inspection agencies that if every one of them comes at least once, then that's it, the company would just fold.

We still have these 'black holes' into which the allocated funds disappear. We repair the same roads over and over, year after year, instead of gradually expanding the amount of high-quality road construction.

I want to once again remind employers about their social responsibility. When restructuring production in single-industry towns, they must always think about the people, taking into account whether the city or district has alternative jobs.

Salaries of executives in publicly funded institutions should be no more than eight times higher than the average salary in that particular institution. This difference is high enough to provide a decent salary to senior executives and recognise their managerial abilities and qualifications. Anything above that is unacceptable.

We must create tax conditions so as to ensure that investing money in Russia is more advantageous than hiding it on some island or spending it on luxury items.

Letting the growth of social spending outstrip the growth of the economy will lead us to a dead end.

Even where I live the water from the pipes is sometimes rusty – it's funny but true. It's shameful to even talk about it, you understand, although it is a government property. Maybe that's why?

The main sources of energy in Russia are non-renewable resources such as oil, natural gas and coal. But these may one day run out. How do you see the energy future of our country?

Vladimir Putin: First of all, it is not going to happen any time soon. We keep on discovering more and more new deposits, confirmed ones at that. As for what will happen, the whole world is working on hydrogen energy, on renewable sources of energy, on bio fuels. Humankind has a wide variety of choices. The challenge is that it should be more efficient and cheaper than hydrocarbons.

I have already quoted one of Saudi Arabia's energy ministers, I like that quote very much: he said the Stone Age ended not because people ran out of stones but because new technologies appeared. It is the same here, new technologies keep springing up, and we must be on top of this progress.

Providing loans at rates that are economically ungrounded is very dangerous. This is akin to printing money, quite simply. After this, it is only a matter of time until a crisis. It would be unavoidable. The same thing happened with mortgage loans in the United States, when banks did not even check the solvency of borrowers and simply handed out huge amounts of money for mortgages.

Those who have stood aside and done nothing are usually rewarded here, while those who are innocent are punished.

No one should be the victim of unfounded accusations. We should not forget about the presumption of innocence. Or are we to treat all people in this country as thieves?

Do you know what the reaction was when I said that I was going to come here? "Don't! Let me show you another plant, built quite recently." Why were they dashing to and fro here, like frightened roaches, just before I arrived? Weren't any competent decision-makers here before, when people could not get their wages for months on end, and the heating was off?

When I moved to Moscow from St. Petersburg I was shocked by how many crooks had gathered here.

Maybe these people did make the money legally. Having made their billions, they spend tens, hundreds of millions of dollars to protect their billions. We know how this money is being spent – to which lawyers, PR campaigns and politicians it is going.

It is difficult to demand public respect for property acquired in corrupt deals.

If you don't swindle people you will not come to the attention of the state.

All bosses want to have the right to issue licenses and permits, sign papers and receive payment for this under the table. That is a traditional Russian scourge.

We recognize that private property and the market economy are much more effective than a planned economy. This means that a private owner runs his or her own company more effectively, but the state creates an economically effective and socially sound tax system, and receives more resources in state revenues to solve social tasks.

If by free press you mean the freedom of individual oligarchs, as they are called, to buy journalists and dictate their will then yes, it is under threat. I don't think we can allow certain individuals to determine the country's strategy at will, stuffing their pockets with illegally-acquired money.

We should give a clear definition of the term "oligarch". If it means big Russian business which is doing spectacularly well through its own efforts – by introducing new goods, new technologies and breaking into new markets, we are all in favour of such business. We are proud of these fellow Russians. They are helping not only themselves but also their colleagues and the country.

But there is a different kind of "businessmen" who sponge on state budget money, enjoy easy-term credits and various exemptions from Russian legislation, in short, they grab state resources. Some of them are trying to use the resources they thus obtain to influence the government and society. We will wage an uncompromising war on such "oligarchs".

Government should be sufficiently strong to be able to guarantee sovereignty, security, and defence capability but it should also be sensitive to regional and municipal issues and sensitive to the needs of individuals. Such government cannot be achieved if citizens do not feel any connection with the state and do not think they have any influence on the authorities, and so government must be democratic. This is very fine and delicate work and we need to be very much aware of what stage of development society has reached, and what is acceptable and what is not possible.

The ultimate goal is the well-being of the people. But that cannot be achieved by just throwing in all our resources. The well-being of the people can only be based on real growth in the economy.

Our partners must know that the colonial method of exploiting Russian resources has no chance.

IV

Everyone is ready to talk about human rights, but of some other country – about their own country nobody wants to discuss this subject.

As far as democracy is concerned, the ruling classes usually talk about freedom to pull the wool over the eyes of those whom they govern.

Geopolitics have always been at the basis of the interests of any state, and remain so.

Twenty-five years ago the Berlin Wall fell, but Europe's division was not overcome, invisible walls simply moved to the East.

United States' attack submarines are concentrated in that area, not far from the Norwegian coast, and the missiles they carry would reach Moscow within 15-16 minutes, just to remind you.

No one is pressuring us, they are trying to, yes, but not from all sides. Their arms are not long enough to reach us from all sides even if they'd like to. It's true though what Alexander Solzhenitsyn said, I cannot remember his exact words, but he said it was time to stand up for Russia because otherwise they'd squeeze us out once and for all.

Russia found itself in a position it could not retreat from. If you compress a spring all the way to its limit, it will snap back hard. You must always remember this.

Edward Snowden is not our agent. He did not give away any secrets, although the rascal really should have given us something – we gave him asylum after all.

If you just think back to childhood when you go into the street with a sweet in your hand and another kid says: "Give it to me". And you clutch your little fist tight around it and say: "And what do I get then?" That is what we want to know – what do we get in return?

Barack Obama: We also compared notes on President Putin's expertise in Judo and my declining skills in basketball.

Vladimir Putin: Mr President wants to weaken me with the statement of his declining skills.

You are right that we have stockpiled more weapons than we need. It does not matter how many times over we can destroy each other.

Take a globe, give it a spin, and point your finger randomly. You will point to a place where the United States has interests and has most likely intervened. I know this from my conversations with almost all leaders and heads of state. They just do not want to fall out with the Americans. No one talks about it openly, but everyone is saying the same thing.

An empire cannot afford to display weakness, and any attempt to strike an agreement on equitable terms is often seen domestically as weakness.

The point is that one side wants to be fully invincible, which upsets the global balance. As soon as one side gets an illusion that it's invincible to a retaliatory strike by the other side, the number of conflicts goes up.

Maybe the United States' exceptional position and the way they are carrying out their leadership really is a blessing for us all, and their meddling in events all around the world is bringing peace, prosperity, progress, growth and democracy, and we should maybe just relax and enjoy it all?

This is the way nouveaux riche behave when they suddenly end up with a great fortune, in this case, in the shape of world leadership and domination. Instead of managing their wealth wisely, for their own benefit too of course, I think they have committed many follies.

Let them go to China and try managing its more than 1.5 billion people. I doubt they would do it better than Mr Hu Jintao.

The entire world remembers the US Secretary of State demonstrating the evidence of Iraq's weapons of mass destruction, waving around some test tube with washing powder in the UN Security Council.

They say there is no democracy in Saudi Arabia either, and it's difficult to disagree with that. Nobody is getting ready to bomb Saudi Arabia.

A well-known person once said: "You can get much further with a kind word and a Smith & Wesson than with just a kind word." Unfortunately, he was right.

Only an insane person and only in a dream can imagine that Russia would suddenly attack NATO.

We can take a confrontational approach and rattle our sabres, try to scare each other, or we can look for compromises and come to agreements.

Many leading armies of the world are switching to ground and air vehicles that have no live operator, no pilot or tank crewperson. This is a very promising direction. There is even an opinion that future conflicts will end when one team of robots beats the other. So that people do not have to suffer.

Maybe it would be best if our bear just sat still. Maybe he should stop chasing pigs and boars around the taiga and start picking berries and eating honey. Maybe then he will be left alone. But no, he won't be! Because someone will always try to chain him up.

The political and economic elites of these countries only like us when we are poor and standing with a begging bowl.

Armed men seized the [Ukrainian] presidential residence. Imagine something like that in the US, if the White House was seized. What would you call that, a coup d'etat? Or say that they just came to sweep the floors.

Historically Crimea is Russian territory where Russians live. They came under threat and there was no way we could abandon them. We were not the ones who carried out the government coup [in Ukraine]. Nationalists and other extremists did. You supported them. But where are you? Thousands of kilometers away. But we are here and this is our land. What do you want to fight for? You don't know? We do know and we are ready to do so.

I can hardly imagine the Ambassador of the Russian Federation to the US actively working with members of the "Occupy Wall Street" movement.

Sanctions should be imposed on those who stage coups and those who help them. As for us, we acted in the interests of Russian people and the country as a whole. Giving this up for money, giving people up for some benefit, for the ability to sign contracts or receive bank transfers, would be absolutely unacceptable.

How long will it last there in the Ukraine? I do not know. It depends on the people living there, on how long they will tolerate it. But I really hope that it will be over one day, and this time, with God's help, it will be over without bloodshed, in the course of democratic processes and the restoration of our natural ties.

Terrorists, like pernicious bacteria, quickly adapt to the organism which hosts them and behave as parasites. They use Western institutions and Western ideas of human rights and the protection of civilians but do this not to develop these ideas or defend Western values and institutions but to fight them.

They are trying to create a Caliphate from Southern Europe to Central Asia.

On no account must you even try to use terrorists to solve your transitory political and even geopolitical tasks. Because if you support them in one place, they will raise their head in another. And they will inevitably strike those who supported them yesterday.

The West is fighting them in Mali, but once they cross the border into Syria, they get support from the West. What is the logic in all of this?

The stationing of Soviet missiles in Cuba was provoked by the stationing of American missiles in Turkey. Khrushchev was not the one who initiated the Cuban Missile Crisis.

One must honestly admit that the former Soviet Union tried to dominate not only Eastern Europe, but many other parts of the world. It did little good to the Russian people and it certainly could not have elicited a positive reaction from our quasi-partners.

The US spends more on defence than all other countries in the world combined.

Everywhere, especially in the United States, the bureaucracy is very strong. And bureaucracy is what rules the world.

The UN has calculated that we've lost around $50-52 billion, and that the countries that imposed the sanctions have lost $100 billion. In other words, sanctions have proven to be a double-edged sword.

We proposed conducting an inspection right there on the airfield from where President Assad's aircraft had allegedly taken off with chemical weapons on board. I would like to reiterate because not everyone has heard this: if chemical weapons had been used, if some shells with toxic agents had been loaded, modern analysers, modern control systems would definitely have detected that there were chemical weapons there on board this aircraft, on that exact spot.

They declined. Nobody wants to. There is a lot of talk but no practical action. We proposed conducting an inspection in the area of the attack, "Let us see what there is." No way again. "Why not?" "It is too dangerous there." "What is so dangerous there if the strike was allegedly carried out against the good part of the armed opposition? These are normal people out there, why would they be dangerous?" "No, it is not possible there either."

I hear this all the time: Russia wants to be respected. Don't you?

We categorically oppose any expansion to the club of nuclear powers, including by North Korea. On the other hand, we understand that recent global developments, in particular blatant violations of international law, invasion of foreign states, regime change and the like, are spurring this arms race.

We know that in the USA and some other places, some hold the view that the worse the relations between Russia and Ukraine, the better it is for them, because it weakens Russia and hampers whichever integration processes that would strengthen Russia, including economically. They would rather see Russia too busy with issues on its borders with its neighbours to be able to stick its nose into international issues such as Syria, the Middle East and others.

The Ukrainian leadership needs money, and the best way to drum up some money is to go to the European Union, individual countries of Europe, the United States, or international financial institutions, posing as a victim of aggression.

You asked me if I was a friend or not. The relations between states are a little different from those between individuals. I am no friend, bride, or groom; I am the President of the Russian Federation.

The only real way to fight international terrorism is to destroy the terrorists in the territory that they have already captured rather than waiting for them to arrive on our soil.

What do you like most about America?

Vladimir Putin: America's creative approach to solving the problems the country is faced with, its openness and open-mindedness which make it possible to unleash the potential of the people. I believe that largely due to these qualities America has made such tremendous strides in its development.

America is a great power, a powerful country, and the Americans are a talented and successful people. There is plenty that we can learn from them.

The struggle for geopolitical interests leads to the situation when a country either becomes stronger, resolving its financial, defence, economic and subsequently social issues more effectively, or slides into the category of third- or fifth-rate countries, losing the possibility of safeguarding the interests of its people.

The South Stream [gas pipeline] project cannot be implemented unilaterally. This is just like love: it can only be happy if there are two people in this wonderful process and both want to develop their relations.

We will react appropriately and proportionately to the approach of NATO's military infrastructure toward our borders.

If they try to punish someone like misbehaving children or to stand them in the corner on a sack of peas or do something to hurt them, eventually they will bite the hand that feeds them.

Capital as such is not patriotic in itself. Capital always flows to where the best conditions exist for its use.

One of the governors [in Ukraine] was chained and handcuffed to something and they poured water over him, in the cold of winter. He was actually only recently appointed to this position, in December, I believe. Even if we accept that they are all corrupt there, he had barely had time to steal anything.

During any sharp turns in world history Russia and the USA have always been together, I mean the First and Second World Wars.

You said that Russia is located between the East and the West. In fact, it is the East and West that are located to the left and right of Russia.

As Alexander III once said, everyone is afraid of our huge size. That is why we have only two allies, the army and the navy.

The Chinese are a smart and cunning people, with a great culture. They know that it is better, as Deng Xiaoping taught, better for now not to stick one's head out.

They say the UN Security Council is ineffective or completely dysfunctional. But the Security Council is not there to rubberstamp decisions that are convenient for one side.

If the fight is inevitable, be the first to strike. And I assure you, the threat of terrorist strikes against Russia has not become greater due to our actions in Syria.

Television channels showed how members of the armed Syrian opposition take out the internal organs of their dead enemies and eat them. I hope that we will not see such negotiators at Geneva 2.

We do not intend to run around the world waving a razor blade, as some people do.

It would be inappropriate to wish problems on any country. We would all be better off living in a prosperous world, rather than in a world of disasters.

I am sure you have great respect for the legal system in the United States. There, just you try to put your hand in your pocket and pull something out – you'll get a bullet in the head and that'll be the end of the discussion. And the police officer will be acquitted.

They have failed to shut Guantanamo for eight years now. They keep people there in shackles and chains without trial or investigation, like in the Middle Ages. Such people are now lecturing us about some of our failings.

Is it right to be an angel at home, a democrat inside your own country and a monster to the rest of the world?

If we are slapped, we must retaliate, otherwise we will always be taken advantage of.

A country's standing is not determined by its size today but by the welfare of its citizens above all, and this is an area where we have a lot to achieve yet.

If those who developed the atomic bomb are ready to renounce it, just as I hope other nuclear powers – official and unofficial would be, then of course we would welcome and facilitate the process in every way possible.

Georgian troops started ground operations, there were numerous losses but nobody said a word. But when the aggressor was hit in the face, when he got his teeth knocked out, when he abandoned all his American weapons and fled as fast as he could, everyone suddenly remembered international law and the evil Russia.

What did you expect us to do, wield a stationery knife there?

What is a unipolar world? However one might embellish this term, at the end of the day it refers to one type of situation, namely one centre of authority, one centre of force, one centre of decision-making. One state and, of course, first and foremost the United States, has overstepped its national borders in every way. This is visible in the economic, political, cultural and educational policies it imposes on other nations. Well, who likes this?

NATO expansion does not have any relation with ensuring security in Europe. On the contrary, it represents a serious provocation that reduces the level of mutual trust. And we have the right to ask: against whom is this expansion intended? And what happened to the assurances our western partners made after the dissolution of the Warsaw Pact?

The stones and concrete blocks of the Berlin Wall have long been distributed as souvenirs. But we should not forget that the fall of the Berlin Wall was possible thanks to a historic choice – one that was also made by our people, the people of Russia – a choice in favour of democracy, freedom, openness and a sincere partnership with all the members of the big European family.

And now they are trying to impose new dividing lines and walls on us – is it possible that we will once again require many years and decades, as well as several generations of politicians, to dismantle these new walls?

There must be a threat so that the US can protect its allies from it.

Today many talk about the struggle against poverty. What is actually happening in this sphere? On the one hand, financial resources are allocated for programmes to help the world's poorest countries – linked with the development of that same donor country's companies. And on the other hand, developed countries simultaneously keep their agricultural subsidies and limit some countries' access to high-tech products. One hand distributes charitable help and the other hand not only preserves economic backwardness but also reaps the profits thereof. The increasing social tension in depressed regions inevitably results in the growth of radicalism and extremism, and feeds terrorism and local conflicts.

I think that it is clear for all, that when these non-governmental organisations are financed by foreign governments, we see them as an instrument that foreign states use to carry out their Russian policies. That is the first thing. The second, in every country there are certain rules for financing, shall we say, election campaigns. Financing from foreign governments, including within governmental campaigns, proceeds through non-governmental organisations. Is this normal democracy? It is secret financing. Hidden from society.

In one part of the world people who fight for independence are called 'fighters for independence', while in another they are called 'separatists' and appeals are made to combat them.

They say they don't mean to kill [Gaddafi], but why bomb his palaces then – to get rid of mice, perhaps?

Journalist: Mrs Clinton said that as a former KGB officer, by definition, you don't have a soul.

Vladimir Putin: At the very least a statesman should have a head.

There are not that many countries in the world today that have the good fortune to say they are sovereign. You can count them on your fingers: China, India, Russia and a few other countries.

Amnesty International has concluded that the United States is now the principal violator of human rights and freedoms worldwide. I have the quote here, I can show you. And there is argumentation behind it.

We all remember what arguments some western countries used to justify their colonial expansion into Africa and Asia. If you look back at the newspapers of those years you will see that what was said then hardly differs from what is being said now in relation to the Russian Federation. You just need to replace the civilising role and civilisation with democratisation and democracy.

The inspectors are working there [in Iraq]. We trust them. They have not found anything; at least they have not yet found anything. The inspectors must continue their work. I am convinced that unilateral actions would be a big mistake. It would radicalize the Islamic world, might well cause a new wave of terrorist acts, and prejudice the leadership of those Muslim countries that are guided by democratic values.

A bad peace is always better than a good war.

The military is always dissatisfied with the money they get from the State.

America will never be Russia and Russia will never be America. But we can complement each other very well and our mutual cooperation is a key factor of world stability. We must never forget that.

Finland has made impressive use of its neutral status and its relations with the Soviet Union, and is today successfully developing its relations with Russia. We really believe that our relations with Finland can set an example for other states, the European Union included, on how to develop relations with Russia.

We must determine our position with regard to the Taliban. It is a known fact that there are bases for training terrorists who act not only against us, but against you too. 6/18/2001

Why hasn't Bin Laden been extradited? It is a challenge to the international community. So far neither Russia nor the world community has reacted to that threat adequately. 12/14/2000

It is always a pleasure to talk about the problems of your neighbours.

As for your question against whom should Russia defend itself, my answer is very simple: against surprises. This, I think, is the aim of the defence policies pursued by the US, France and other states. The more predictable and fair the international order, the less states will have to spend on their security.

Why should we be happy about Nato expanding and coming closer to our borders? Of course it is causing us concern.

Contemporary Russia does not view anybody as an enemy nor even as an opponent. We would like, at a minimum, to have partnership relations with everybody.

If you want to live well yourself, you should also want your neighbours to live well.

Of course, there are people in the West who will always criticise us and take an anti-Russian stand out of geopolitical considerations.

After the notorious McCarthyism period [in the US], the leftist movement was eliminated there.

No foreign country with a sense of self-respect allows the use of foreign money in internal politics. Try and do something like this in the US and you'll land in jail at once.

Do not blame the mirror when your mug is crooked.

A former European leader told me, "What kind of democracy is it in the US – you cannot even consider running in an election if you don't have a billion, or even several billion dollars!"

Let's take the lobbying for private corporations – what is it, is it corruption or not? It's legalised and so formally is okay, within the law. But that depends on how you look at it.

The ability to manipulate public opinion is no less in western countries, the so-called developed democracies, than it is here.

Any state is by nature a huge and lazy animal.

Very often people's perception of the whole state greatly depends on how policemen treat citizens.

If you want to become an Islamic radical and are ready to be circumcised, I invite you to Moscow. We are a multi-faith country and we have experts who can do it. And I would advise them to carry out that operation in such a way that nothing would grow in that place again.

We'll chase the terrorists everywhere – in the airport. We'll catch them in the toilet and waste them.

There is always a fine line between what I described as a dangerous desire to shock and freedom of artistic expression. These activists, in a manner of speaking, went to the Charlie Hebdo editorial offices and shot people. Did those cartoonists have to insult Muslims? They took the publication as an insult. It is another matter perhaps that the artists did not mean to insult anybody, but they did. No matter what, we must not allow the situation to get to this point and divide society.

Let's rely on our own experience, the European experience now is not the best. Listen, in general it is stupidity there. You saw what is happening, an immigrant raped a child in one of the European countries. The court acquitted him on two grounds: he spoke the language of the host country badly and didn't understand that the boy, and it was a boy, was objecting. It wouldn't even occur to you what they are doing there. It's the result of the erosion of traditional national values and – I don't even know how to explain – feelings of guilt towards these migrants. It's even incomprehensible what the problem is there. But a society that can't defend its children today won't have a future tomorrow.

[Western media] will continue blindly repeating what they've been told to say, what they've been paid to say. They are just doing their work.

Western media create a parallel reality with regard to events in Ukraine. What is that? It is an order from the authorities, and the media are carrying out that political order. I suppose we have something similar in certain areas. Is that good or bad? It's bad. If the press wants people to believe it, it should remain objective.

When people see and know that the government cares about its senior citizens, they treat their country and their government differently; they even plan their lives differently, in the sense that there is a reliable system of state support and care for people. And this always creates internal stability in any nation, in any society.

Everything goes through servers located in the United States, everything is monitored there.

Global changes occur at all times – simply at different rates. In the Middle Ages, there was one rate of change and in our days it is significantly higher, which has to do with the accumulation of knowledge. The more knowledge mankind has, the faster the changes. First, there is accumulation and then there is a leap. So it seems that we are now on the threshold of a leap.

Many European countries are witnessing a rise of a dependency mentality when not working is often much more beneficial than working. This type of mentality endangers not only the economy but also the moral basis of society. It is no secret that many citizens of less developed countries come to Europe intentionally to live off welfare.

There is only one way [to fight religious extremism]: to enhance the prosperity of the Muslim population or Muslim countries generally and to introduce universal human values.

Our eco-system is very vulnerable. It is amazing that the Earth still survives today. Our planet evolved through a combination of billions of circumstances and continues to exist thanks to the fact these billions of circumstances somehow interact and work together. Our planet, which is in constant movement through what is essentially the hostile environment of outer space, is faced with the constant threat of destruction. It could be hit by large cosmic bodies. We have a very thin ozone layer and our atmosphere in general is really quite thin. There is a very fine line beyond which damage becomes irreversible, and we might not even notice that we have crossed this line.

We know them very well, they are very intelligent people, attractive, well-educated and know how to speak well and correctly lay out their position, and that always sounds very convincing, liberal, and market-oriented. But to agree with them so that they concede even one millimeter is impossible unless in response we have to concede at minimum half a meter of our interests.

After the well-known events in Cyprus and with the on-going sanctions campaign, our business has finally realised that its interests abroad are not reckoned with and that it can even be fleeced like a sheep.

The American economy will recover in the short and medium term, there is no doubt about it. Of course, we do not know what will happen later if they continue to pursue the same careless economic policy as in the previous years.

Europe deserves credit for having made more effort to give a social dimension to its economy, and so the divides are not as great there. I think therefore that we would do well to study Europe's best practice and traditions in this area and see what we can try out here at home.

Genuine democracy can be established only as a result of the internal development of society itself.

Globalisation should not make the poor still poorer and the rich still richer.

Appendix: US Elections

I used to have a lot of discussions with my American colleagues. I would say: how come the majority of the population voted for one person, but got quite another as president? Through the Electoral College system. The Americans responded: Don't get into it, we're used to it and it'll stay like that. 10 June 2010

The USA, as we all know, is in the middle of an election campaign, and it is very tempting at such times to notch up some points by making hardline statements and playing on old ideological stereotypes and phobias that it is high time we abandoned. July 9, 2012

Just imagine if we were to write into Russian law that our goal is to democratise the United States. October 22, 2015

[On Donald Trump] He's a very bright person, and talented, without any doubt. But it's not our business to determine his qualities – that's up to the American voters. December 17, 2015

First Bush Sr. was in power there, later on Bush Jr. – all from the same family. Clinton was in power for two terms and now his wife is laying claim to this position, and the family may remain in office. What does this have to do with turnover? As the saying goes, "Husband and wife are a single devil," and they will be at the helm. I am not saying this is all bad. There are pros and cons to it. April 14, 2016

It is regrettable to see that the Russian card gets played the way it does during nearly every US election campaign. June 17, 2016

What are we witnessing? Some hackers published information about the unseemly conduct of Ms Clinton's campaign headquarters – supporting one candidate for the party nomination at the expense of the other. Hysterical accusations were made that this is in Russia's interest. But there is nothing in Russia's interest there. They freak out about it to distract the attention of the American people from the importance of what was published. October 12, 2016

Does anyone seriously imagine that Russia can somehow influence the American people's choice? America is not some kind of 'banana republic', after all, but is a great power. Do correct me if I am wrong.

We do not know what Mr Trump would do if he wins, and we do not know what Ms Clinton would do. Overall then, it does not really matter to us who wins. Of course we can only welcome public words about a willingness to normalise relations between our two countries.

Mr Trump behaves extravagantly, of course, we all see this. But I think there is some sense in his actions. I say this because in my view he represents the interests of the sizeable part of American society that is tired of the elites that have been in power for decades now.
October 27, 2016

I want to congratulate the American people on the end of this election cycle and congratulate Mr Donald Trump on his victory in the election. We heard the statements he made as candidate for president expressing a desire to restore relations between our countries. We realise and understand that this will not be an easy road given the level to which our relations have degraded today, regrettably. November 9, 2016

We are seeing the continuation of an acute internal political struggle despite the fact that the presidential election is over and it ended in Mr Trump's convincing victory. Nevertheless, in my opinion, several goals are being set in this struggle. The first is to undermine the legitimacy of the US president-elect. The second goal is to tie the new president's hands as he works to fulfil the campaign promises he made to the American people.

Look, I am not acquainted with Mr Trump. I have never met him. I do not know what he will do in the international arena, so I have no reason either to attack him or criticise him for whatever reason or to defend him, no matter what. We will not even ask the Nobel Committee to give him a Nobel Prize.

When Mr Trump came to Moscow a few years ago – I don't remember exactly when – he was not a politician. We were unaware of his political ambitions. He was just a businessman to us, one of the wealthiest men in America. Does anyone think that our special services are chasing after every American billionaire? Of course not. It's nonsense. That's my first point.

Second, concerning the allegation that Trump arrived in Moscow and the first thing he did was meet with

Moscow prostitutes. First, he is an adult and, second, he has for many years sponsored beauty contests and had the chance to meet the world's most beautiful women. Why would he run to a hotel to meet up with our girls of limited social responsibility? Although they are, of course, the best in the world.
January 17, 2017

They are using anti-Russian slogans to destabilize the internal political situation in the United States, but they do not realise that they are harming their own country. If this is the case, then they are quite simply stupid. If they do understand what they are doing, then they are dangerous and unscrupulous people. In any event, this is the United States' own affair and we have no intention of getting involved. May 17, 2017

I have already spoken to three US Presidents. They come and go, but politics stay the same at all times. Do you know why? Because of the powerful bureaucracy. When a person is elected, they may have some ideas. Then people with briefcases arrive, well dressed, wearing dark suits, just like mine, except for the red tie, since they wear black or dark blue ones. These people start explaining how things are done. And instantly, everything changes. This is what happens with every administration. May 31, 2017

Hackers are free people like artists. If artists get up in the morning feeling good, all they do all day is paint. The same goes for hackers. They got up today and read that something is going on internationally. If they are feeling patriotic they will start contributing, as they believe, to the justified fight against those speaking ill of Russia. Is that possible? In theory, yes. At the government level, we never engage in this. This is what is most important. June 1, 2017

I have read these [US intelligence] reports. There is nothing specific. There is only supposition and inference. That is it. You know, if there is anything specific, then there will be something to discuss. As they used to say in the organisation where I worked at one time: "addresses, safe houses, names." So, where is all that?

Somebody is behind this. The people who engage in this nonsense also initiate such reports. I think this needs to come to an end, and the sooner, the better. It is necessary to begin normal cooperation.

IP addresses can be simply made up. Do you know how many such specialists there are? They will make it look like it was sent from your home address by your children – your three-year old kid, they will organise everything to look like it was your three-year old daughter who carried out the attack. There are such IT specialists in the world today and they can arrange anything and then blame it on whomever.

Trump's team proved more capable during the election campaign. At times, I actually thought the man was overdoing it, really. That is true. However, it turned out that he was right, that he found a key to those social groups and voters' groups that he had bet on, and they came out and voted for him.

The other team lost. They are reluctant to acknowledge the mistake. They do not want to admit that they did not get it, that they miscalculated. It is easier to say, "We are not to blame, the Russians are to blame, they interfered in our election, but we are good." It reminds me of anti-Semitism: the Jews are to blame for everything. The halfwit cannot do anything but the Jews are the ones who are to blame. However, we know what such sentiments can lead to.

You have just mentioned disinformation. What disinformation? One of the hackers' planted stories was that Mrs Clinton's election campaign managers had acted unfairly with regard to other Democratic Party candidates. However, when that information appeared in the public domain, the campaign manager actually acknowledged that it was true and resigned. Is that disinformation? It is truthful information.

Does it really matter who revealed it? They should have apologised to the public and they should have said before resigning, "We will not repeat these mistakes." But what did they do? They said, "We are not to blame. It is the Russians." What have the Russians got to do with it? Did the Russians engage in pushing through one Democratic Party candidate to the detriment of another candidate? Whatever the case might be, we did not do it.

As for interference, you should have seen what your colleagues are doing here. They have simply barged into our internal politics with their shoes on. They are walking all over us, chewing gum. They are just having fun. This is systematic, years-long, gross, absolutely unceremonious interference in our domestic policy, including the level of diplomatic missions. Let us end this. You will feel better, and we will feel better.

Our ambassador met with someone. What should an ambassador do? That is his job. That is what he gets paid for. He should have meetings, discussing current affairs, reaching agreements.

I saw that President Trump then fired his aide because he was accused of talking to somebody somewhere. There were simply general words about the need to think about how to develop our relations. Should we not think about developing our relations, or what? Should we simply act on the spur of the moment?
June 2, 2017

If we were to discuss some kind of political and social justice, then the [US]· electoral legislation probably needs to be changed to bring about a situation where the head of state is elected by direct secret ballot so there will be a direct tabulation of votes that can be easily monitored. That's all there is to it. And there will be no need for those who have lost the elections to point fingers and blame their troubles on anybody. June 5, 2017

There is a theory that Kennedy's assassination was arranged by the United States special services. If this theory is correct, and one cannot rule it out, so what can be easier in today's context, being able to rely on the entire technical capabilities available to special services, than to organise some kind of attacks in the appropriate manner while making a reference to Russia in the process. June 5, 2017

Greetings, Mr Putin. My name is Jeremy Bowling. As an American who sits here in America and sees the racist Russian phobia running crazy in my country, what advice would you give me to help set the record straight, to help my fellow Americans understand that Russia is not the enemy?

Vladimir Putin: To begin with, I am very grateful to you for this call. And I can tell you as the current head of the

Russian state that I know the attitudes of our people. We do not consider America our enemy. Moreover, twice in history when we were going through very hard times, we pooled our efforts; we were allies in two world wars. In the past, the Russian Empire played a substantial role in helping America gain independence and supported the United States. We see that Russophobia is running high in America and think this is primarily a result of the escalating political infighting.

I do not think I have the right to give you any advice. I simply want to thank you for this stance. We know that we have very many friends in the United States. My American colleagues told me so, and public opinion polls show the same results. At any rate, those polls taken a month ago show that we have many friends there. True, regrettably such hysteria is bound to affect the frame of mind, but let me assure you that there are also very many people in Russia who have deep respect for the achievements of the American people and are hoping that eventually our relations will get back on track, in which both we and the United States are extremely interested.
June 15, 2017

The former FBI director said that he believes that Russia interfered in the US election process. He did not provide any evidence, as usual, but he said there were attempts "to shape the way we think, vote, and act." Is that not the way it is all over the world?

Next, he said quite unexpectedly that he had written down a conversation with the President, and then passed along this conversation to the media through a friend. It sounds and looks very strange when the head of an intelligence agency writes down a conversation with the commander-in-chief, and then passes it to the media through a friend. How then is the FBI director different from Mr Snowden? In that case, he is not the head of an intelligence agency, but a human rights activist who takes a certain position.

By the way, if he is persecuted in any way for this, we will be willing to grant him political asylum in Russia as well. He should know that.
June 15, 2017

[On Donald Trump] He is quite an open person and he is very different from the TV image that he created during the election campaign. However, there is nothing unusual here, since the election campaign is not something you judge a person by. An election campaign requires a special mind-set and behaviour.

What I also noticed and could share with you – he has the ability to listen. I do not know what he is like with other people he talks to, but during our conversation I listened to him with attention when he set out his ideas and proposals on developing cooperation and he did the same. You know, this is something that does not happen all the time.

There are some people who only hear themselves, whatever you tell them – it is like a buzz in the background for them. You are talking to them, but they are not listening at all. The current US President is different: he responds to what his interlocutor says. Even if he does not like something or does not agree with something, he asks questions and responds to arguments. This is very important. And if this dialogue between us continues in this way on the interpersonal level, there is reason to hope that our communication will further develop.
July 14, 2017

The transnational character of US legislation is unacceptable. We have never accepted it and will not accept it. As for the reaction of other states of the world, it depends on the extent of their sovereignty and readiness to defend their own national interests. The sanctions are absolutely illegal from the perspective of international law. July 27, 2017

The US side has carried out a wholly unprovoked, which is very important, step in the deterioration of Russian-US relations: through unlawful restrictions, and through attempts to influence other countries of the world, including its allies, who are interested in developing and maintaining relations with Russia.

We waited for quite some time that maybe something would change for the better. We entertained the hope that the situation would somehow change. But all indications are that, if it changes, it won't be soon. I thought that it was time to show that we won't leave anything unanswered. More than 1,000 [US embassy] employees, including diplomats and technical workers, have been working until now in Russia; 755 will have to cease their activities in the Russian Federation.

We have repeatedly proposed cooperation with the US to secure both our and American interests and in general to bring under control throughout the world such negative activities as cyber crime. Instead of beginning to work constructively, we only hear groundless accusations of interference in the internal affairs of the United States.
July 30, 2017

www.ingramcontent.com/pod-product-compliance
Lightning Source LLC
Chambersburg PA
CBHW051224250726
48655CB00006B/2584